T0210110

Horacio Sanchez Salinas

AuthorHouse™
1663 Liberty Drive
Bloomington, IN 47403
www.authorhouse.com
Phone: 1 (800) 839-8640

Published by AuthorHouse 09/14/2018

ISBN: 978-1-5462-6023-3 (sc)
ISBN: 978-1-5462-6022-6 (e)

Library of Congress Control Number: 2018910892

Print information available on the last page.

authorHOUSE®

For those who believe, and for those who do not.

For those who dream, and for those who follow their dreams.

To Vera, Constanza, Andres, and Almudena.

To Cecilia, Patricio, and Fernanda.

To Pata.

To Family and Friends.

P2 - R001

Leaving a legacy for future generations of supply chain professionals.

Contents

P3 - R001

Introduction

The Supply Chain Playbook is for high school students at all levels around the world who may want to consider exploring supply chain as a career. It is also for people interested in learning about the fascinating world of supply chain and how products are sourced (bought) and then distributed and delivered to stores, projects, or clients around the world. Supply chain is a discipline that is getting a lot of attention, and although you may not know it, it plays a key role in all our lives. The bulk of *The Supply Chain Playbook* is devoted to explaining the origins of supply chain, discussing why supply chain is a key element in today's economy, and outlining the stages of supply chain, strategic sourcing, warehousing, and distribution (logistics). I also analyze the revolutionary effect of supply chain on the food industry, in retail, and on the engineering and construction industry.

The reason the title of this work is "The Supply Chain Playbook" is that strategies in supply chain are very similar to what you see in sports. In the same way that in a game it is important to anticipate the next play, be creative, and innovate, it is necessary to do these things as a supply chain professional.

Supply chain is recognized as a complex network that involves the relationships and activities between producers, distributors, and consumers. Supply chain has diverse definitions, and it is managed and implemented in diverse ways. Each industry customizes its supply chain area based on the organization strategy and customers' requirements. In the food industry, for example, supply chain is more complex because food must meet regulations for how it is managed, stored, and distributed. In retail (department stores, warehouses, discount stores), the supply chain does not have to meet the regulations of the food industry, but products need to be sourced and

distributed on time to maintain stock levels and make it into the hands of consumers. In the engineering and construction industry, supply chain is focused on the acquisition, transportation, and delivery of equipment and materials to projects around the world.

As a supply chain professional, I face all kinds of situations. Some of these situations require effective solutions and decisions that depend on years of expertise and skill development. Supply chain is a discipline where you never stop learning, as it is undergoing constant innovation to meet demanding market trends and customer expectations.

Supply chain requires a new generation of professionals with contemporary skills. I invite you to explore and understand the supply profession and consider it as an option for your future. If you decide to follow this career or discipline, do it with passion and respect. It is a profession that requires constant learning, development of skills, and evolution. It requires commitment to reach excellence, to think differently, and to innovate. In any industry, supply chain is going to give you the opportunity to face difficult challenges or scenarios. You cannot be the best if you do not face the type of situations that will force you to use all your skills, expertise, and knowledge.

The Supply Chain Playbook includes a glossary of professional supply chain terms to facilitate the understanding of concepts and ideas.

How Might We? Is a question that opens a thinking channel to find solutions.

The Origins of Supply Chain

As research and studies have shown, supply chain started with the beginning of civilization and commerce. It was not always called "supply chain," but the activities of selling, transporting, and obtaining raw materials and negotiating are now part of the supply chain discipline. The introduction of currency, whether paper money or gold, silver, or bronze, facilitated commerce around the world. Prehistoric tribes traded food, tools, goods, or animal skins. Aztec emperor Moctezuma liked to eat fresh fish caught daily from the ocean 250 miles away from the Aztec capital.

Inventions like the wheel and vessels (ships) helped in the development of commerce. Ancient Egypt is recognized as the first culture to use ships to transport goods, armies, and people. In ancient China, trade routes (e.g., the Silk Route) were established for commerce between empires. Diverse merchandise traveled along the Silk Route, which stretched from China to India, Asia Minor, Mesopotamia, Egypt, Africa, Greece, Rome, and Britain.

Commerce was not always fair or expeditious, and for that reason it was required to establish rules, procedures, and mechanisms to facilitate trade around the world.

It is difficult to identify a specific period when supply chain emerged as a discipline. Diverse literature identifies supply chain as a profession back in the beginning of the Industrial Revolution. Consumers (people and merchants) demanded more products and better delivery, which forced manufacturers, producers (farms and factories), and retailers to increase efficiency in production and distribution.

The Concept of Supply Chain

Supply chain can be understood as a system where the relationships between the system's components in an organization improve competitiveness and efficiency through improved quality, reduced costs, and the meeting of schedule objectives. Supply chain needs to work as a whole concept, with all areas dependent on others, to avoid any gap in the process that otherwise can affect the entire operation.

Supply chain can also be defined as the following:

- the acquisition and distribution of goods (products)
- the process of requesting pricing for a product and negotiating delivery, terms of payment, and warranty
- the process of acquiring raw materials, manufacturing a product, distributing the product to sales channels, and delivering it to customers
- a network of relationships and activities.

Supply chain in the past was a necessary task but was not a recognized element of global corporations. Now it is a discipline that plays a significant role in the progress of different industries. Supply chain requires execution procedures and strategies that serve as guidelines to bring consistency to the function. It also requires individuals to perform the activities vital to the process. Supply chain teams are a mix of diverse individuals with expertise in purchasing, negotiation, commercial and legal terminology, logistics, quality surveillance, and warehousing.

Philosophy in Supply Chain

Philosophy in simple terms is the study of knowledge and thinking. Through different theories like critical theory, positivism, and hermeneutics, philosophy has contributed enormously to politics, science, literature, and supply chain. The relationship between philosophy and the aforementioned areas of theory as applied to the methodologies used in supply chain is very strong. Critical theory emphasizes the importance of learning from experience to redesign our future. Positivism underlines the importance of having measurable evidence before decisions are made, and hermeneutics emphasizes the importance of interpretation and how people interpret different situations in different ways.

Critical Theory in Supply Chain

In supply chain, critical theory is used to create methodologies that help to find ways to minimize risk for the organizations and clients. The process starts with the identification of the critical path that could lead to significant impacts. To determine the critical path for a project, supply chain managers identify the sequence of tasks and select which ones are going to take more time to be completed. In addition, the time line for each project includes a series of hold points to manage the risk of unexpected problems or impacts. If required, the hold point adds extra time or resources to a specific task or tasks designated on the critical path time line. Provisions for additional costs are also normally included in the budget.

Hermeneutics in Supply Chain

It is valid to say that hermeneutics is a word not commonly used in supply chain. However, hermeneutics is normally involved in the interpretation of terms or in how two different people or more may understand the same situation in different ways.

The supply chain process starts when a requisition to purchase is received. Then it becomes a contractual document between two or more parties, which is when hermeneutics comes into play. With hermeneutics being the science of interpretation, all parties involved in the execution of the contract will try to understand and interpret the scope of the contract, and their respective responsibilities and obligations. It is also common during the negotiation phase to have legal teams trying to understand and interpret terms and conditions that will govern the contract. Hermeneutics is also a key element in the definition, analysis, improvement, and control of different supply chain methodologies.

Positivism in Supply Chain

Positivism in supply chain is generally associated with the analysis and implementation of quantitative methods. Forecasting, planning and scheduling, cost control, and inventory control are quantitative methods related to supply chain. Their function is to identify and implement strategies to solve problems in the context of the different supply chain activities. Forecasting is an activity defined as the effort performed to asses or predict future situations and events (based on historical data). Planning is an activity in charge of the identification of objectives and activities required to finalize the different phases or challenges in a project. Scheduling is focused on applying the duration of each activity.

Cost control involves the application of procedures aiming to follow the financial progress of projects and manufacturing operations to minimize cost, increase profitability, and ensure efficient operations. Inventory control is an activity that manages and tracks materials or goods that are physically available for allocation and are stored and controlled in a warehouse. Inventory control requires the use of quantitative methods to calculate inventory turnover ratios, reorder levels or safety stock.

Procedures and Strategies in Supply Chain

Procedures and strategies are the instructions that supply chain professionals need to follow to perform their jobs in the most productive and efficient way. Both describe the detailed execution approach for each activity, area, or function associated with the planning, definition, quantification, acquisition, and control of goods, and both support the achievement of key objectives and meeting client and market expectations. All organizations are forced to perform the supply chain activities in an ethical manner and in compliance with laws and regulations, using sound business practices from approved sources, which provide maximum value for each expenditure, taking into consideration quality, price, schedule, reliability, safety, and applicable laws.

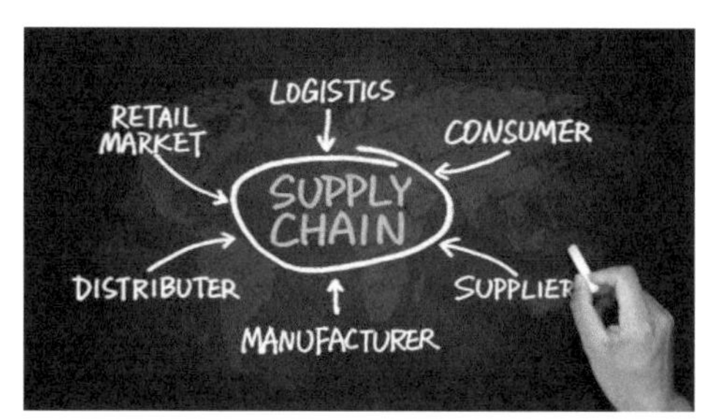

P10 - R001

The Stages of the Supply Chain

There are five stages of the supply chain, which are as follows:

1. Strategic sourcing
   - Development of purchasing plans and strategies
   - Selection of suppliers
   - Purchasing
2. Manufacturing
   - Customer service
   - Expediting
   - Quality surveillance
3. Warehousing
4. Distribution – Logistics
5. Delivery

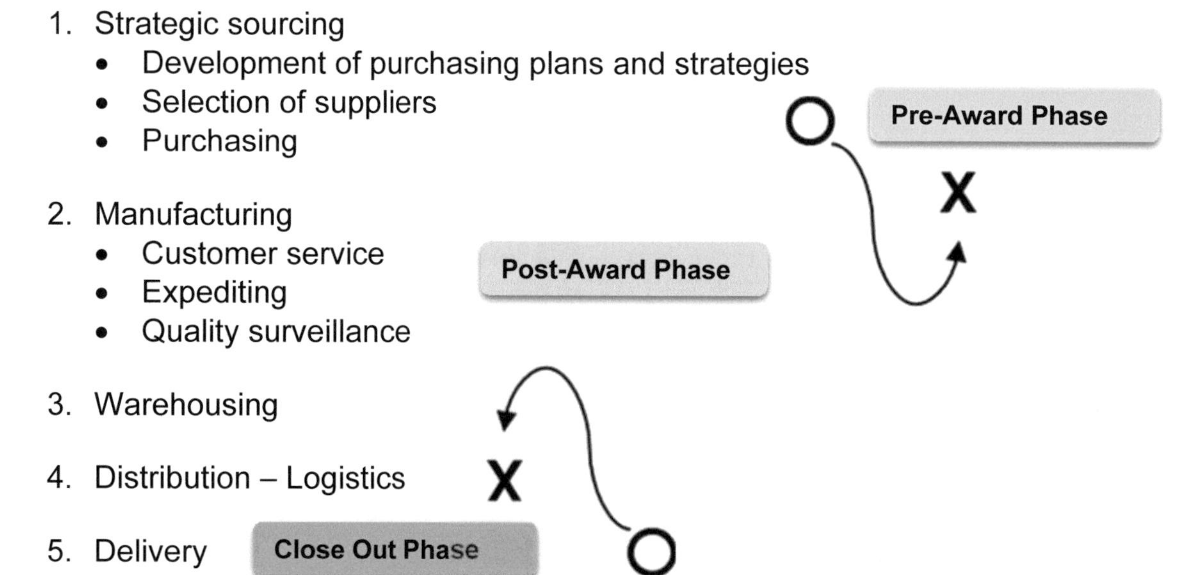

1. Strategic Sourcing

Strategic sourcing is an integral part of the supply chain function that helps to identify cost-competitive strategies. Through market analysis, verification, and certification of vendors, strategic sourcing builds better relationships with vendors around the world to obtain benefits like cost reduction, better availability of products, extension of warranties, post–contract award extended services. Strategic sourcing is also used to identify gaps or areas of opportunity, identify market trends, analyze what competitors are doing, and improve processes to reduce waste.

Development of Purchasing Plans and Strategies

Plans or strategies describe the execution approach for each of the integrated functions associated with the acquisition of products and establish the responsibilities, obligations, and requirements to meet the goals or objectives.

Selection of Suppliers

Buyers, in conjunction with professionals in other areas or disciplines, develop lists of potential suppliers for each product or commodity. Selected vendors normally meet the following criteria: strategic sourcing recommendation, client recommendation, verified and successful vendors, and previous experience.

Purchasing

Once a requirement has been identified, buyers or supply chain managers begin the acquisition or purchasing activity that normally involves the following activities:

a. Request for quotation (RFQ)
b. Evaluation of proposals (bid summary)
c. Terms and conditions
d. Negotiation
e. Recommendation and award purchase order (PO)
f. Change orders
g. Postaward follow-up and closeout
h. Supply chain systems software technology

The buyers perform purchasing tasks in accordance with established techniques, procedures, and criteria. Buyers are also responsible for doing the following:

- developing a package bidders list
- preparing and issuing requests for quotation
- evaluating quotations and preparing bid evaluations for project approval
- conditioning supplier bids and negotiating with suppliers
- preparing, issuing, and administering purchase orders and change orders
- verifying invoice progress payments, discrepancies. and final payment with accounting
- performing closeout on purchase order files
- completing a supplier performance evaluation.

a) Request for Quotation (RFQ)

The RFQ is the action that starts the purchasing process. It is a document (hard copy or electronic) that details the scope of supply and requirements of the goods (materials, equipment, commodities, or services that are required). If, for example, the requirement

of a client or an organization is to buy chairs, the vendor or manufacturer needs to know the quantity, color, size, model, and material.

b) Evaluation of Proposals (Bid Summary)

The RFQ is normally sent to three or more suppliers to guarantee competitive bids and to obtain enough data to help buyers better compare pricing, delivery times, warranty terms, quality systems, and vendor experience. The buyer reviews each bidder's proposal for commercial completeness, price condition, currency, freight terms, shipping point, quoted delivery, transit time, and ETA (estimated time of arrival).

c) Terms and Conditions

All commercial transactions are subject to terms and conditions that regulate both parties (buyer and seller) and guarantee they are following fair rules and regulations. The most common terms are warranty (thirty, sixty, or ninety days, or one or two years), delays, cancellation, returns, refunds, changes, and insurance.

In some cases, the RFQ is sent to only one supplier. In this case, it is called sole or single source.

Single Source: Purchase a product from a selected vendor although other vendors are available.

Sole Source: A product is only available from one vendor.

Buyers or supply chain managers clarify with vendors their proposals and, if necessary, have face-to-face meetings.

d) Negotiation

Negotiation is probably the most interesting phase of the purchasing process. Buyers and sellers try to reach an agreement in terms of payment, delivery, warranty, service, preventive or corrective maintenance, and commercial and legal terms. There is no specific rule on how to negotiate; supply chain professionals need to learn different negotiation tactics because each case requires a different approach.

The first step is to identify needs and goals. What are your goals? For some companies or in some industries, delivery is a key factor, and as a result the buyer is open to paying a premium in the event that the supplier delivers on time or before the agreed date. In other cases, budget limitations increase the difficulty of the negotiation. Supply chain professionals need to develop negotiation skills, control emotions, read nonverbal communication from others, and learn how to use or balance different tactics to face different negotiation challenges and find value.

The most common negotiation tactics are collaboration, competition, accommodation, compromise, and avoidance.

1. Collaboration

This is a win-win approach in which both negotiating parties are open to and interested in reaching a fair agreement. It is a scenario in which ideas, innovation, and mutual commitment work together to build trust between parties that have one common goal.

2. Competition

This is the most used tactic in negotiating. It requires skills and tactics if one is to get the best benefit out of it. This tactic is used when results are needed quickly or when one of the parties has specific goals or needs. The result is usually “I win, you lose.”

3. Accommodation

Negotiators who use this style believe that achieving a goal requires the giving up of benefits in order to get something in return at some point. The result here is “I lose, you win”.

4. Compromise

This tactic is based on trust and the interest to maintain a good relationship. Both parties understand that to reach an agreement, they will have to give up some things. The result of this tactic is “I win some, I lose some; you win some, you lose some.”

5. Avoidance

This tactic is normally a deal breaker, as all communication between the negotiating parties stops. However, the buyer or seller will try to find a way to get something back by contacting others. This is a lose-lose situation.

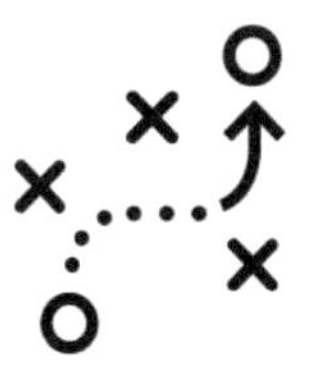

P16 - R001

Negotiating is a learning process, and as such, it is important and recommended that, the negotiator documents all negotiations and implements metrics or use performance indicators. Performance indicators are tools that can contribute to improvements in the supply chain process. A measuring tool can weigh the objectives and the variables that affect the accomplishment of the discipline goals. The difference between the objective value and the measured value is called deviation. The key is to correct or eliminate the variations. A method or strategy that it is commonly used in organizations is the key performance indicator (KPI). Key performance indicators (KPIs) provide ways to measure the performance of business processes internally, with others, or externally.

Metrics help to identify ways to reduce procurement cycle times and involve the activities that deal with how requisitions for purchase (RFQs) and purchase orders (POs) are processed throughout the system and completed. Experienced supply chain professionals use KPI value trees to gain a complete perspective of the processes and variables that affect procurement cycle times. KPI value trees provide an overview of the existing internal and external conditions of the organization or discipline and project any risks that may affect the strategy and goals.

P17 - R001

KPI value trees focus by deconstructing processes in the organization to find the causes for not meeting expectations. The tree is built with a dependent variable as a start point (strategy), and then it opens in "branches" or levels of independent variables that affect the dependent variable (i.e., the KPIs).

e) Recommendation and Award – Purchase Order (PO)

Once the analysis of the proposals is complete, the buyer moves to the recommendation and award phase. It is important to emphasize that the lowest bid or proposal is not always the best option. Some industries focus on a "buy cheap" strategy; however, in the end, this option brings more problems than satisfaction. The key is to find the best overall value—which vendor will give you the best for the money you are going to pay.

Buyers issue a purchase order (PO) to sellers that confirms the deal and states the agreed terms and options.

f) Change Orders

A change order is a document requesting a scope of change or correction. It must be approved and accepted by the buyer and supplier before it can become a legal change to the purchase order. When revising an order, the buyer should review the purchase order and any previous change orders. An accurate summary of the previous scope and changes is mandatory.

g) Postaward Follow-Up and Closeout

Once the product is received, the buyer moves to the post award phase. In this phase, the buyer verifies that the product complies with the requirements, the seller confirms full payment, and the purchase order is closed.

Supply Chain Request for Quotation (RFQ) and Purchase Order (PO) Typical Workflow

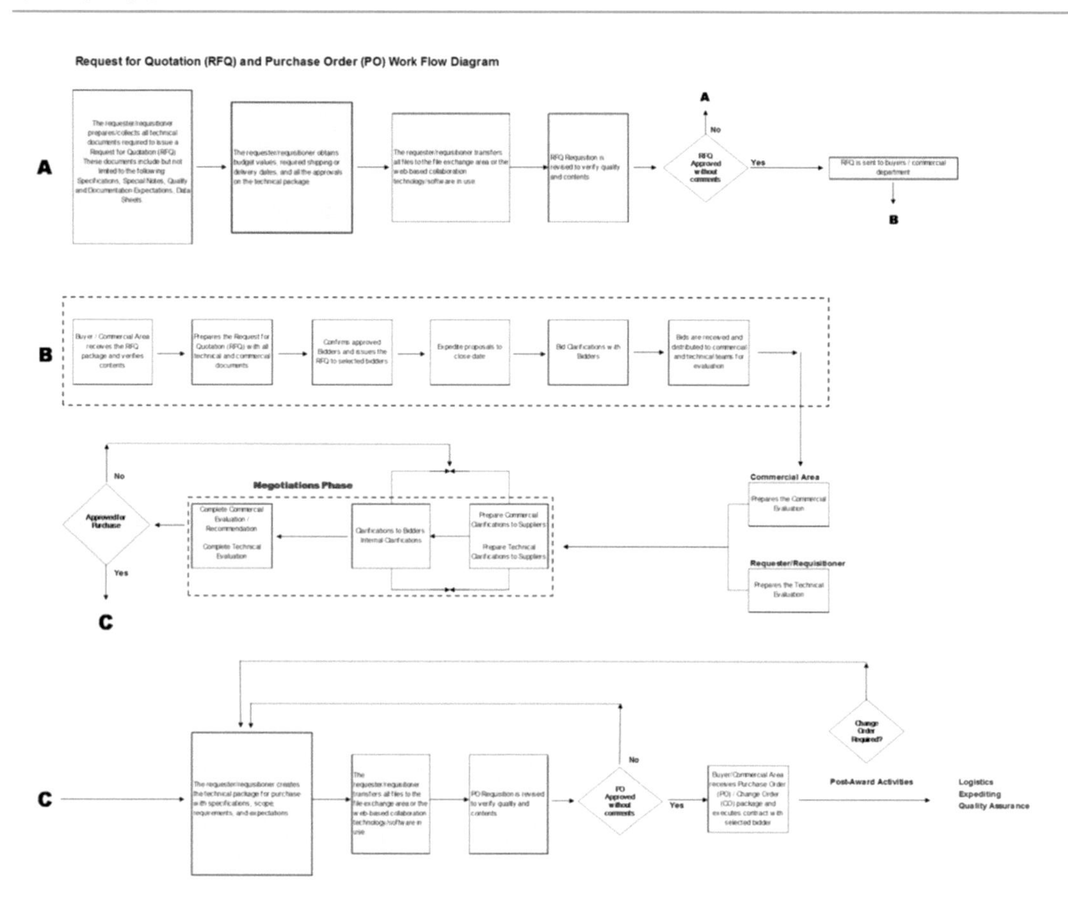

Workflow Dimensions

Dimension **A**

- RFQ technical/specifications package is created.
- RFQ technical package is verified.
- RFQ technical package is transmitted to commercial/other areas as required through established electronic/software methods.

Dimension **B**

- Buyer / Commercial Area receives the RFQ package and verifies contents
- Buyer / Commercial Area Prepares the Request for Quotation (RFQ) with all technical and commercial documents
- RFQ to selected bidders is issued
- Bid Clarifications with Bidders
- Bids are received and distributed to commercial and technical teams for evaluation
- Bids are evaluated and negotiated.
- Recommendation for Award is approved.

Dimension **C**

- The requester/requisitioner creates the technical package for purchase with specifications, scope, requirements, and expectations.
- PO Requisition is revised to verify quality and contents
- Buyer/Commercial Area receives Purchase Order (PO) and executes contract with selected bidder
- Post-Award Activities (Expediting, Quality Assurance, Logistics)

h) Supply Chain Systems Software Technology

Technology and innovation are now recognized as key factors that help to improve results and recognition in the marketplace. This change to a constant evolution mentality has “prompted a renewed emphasis” on capturing value from the implementation and management of new technologies and innovations. In Supply Chain, new technology makes a huge impact on the distribution of goods and services to consumers around the world. For project-based organizations, innovation and technology are now the driving factors of competition.

In supply chain, software solutions and tools (apps, tablets, bar coding, and GPS) help organizations manage and control their daily supply chain operations and help them maintain good relationships with clients and suppliers.

Some organizations used to develop their own in-house software tools that at one point provided a competitive advantage. However, with the current technology and market dynamics, in-house systems are now obsolete, inefficient, and expensive to maintain.

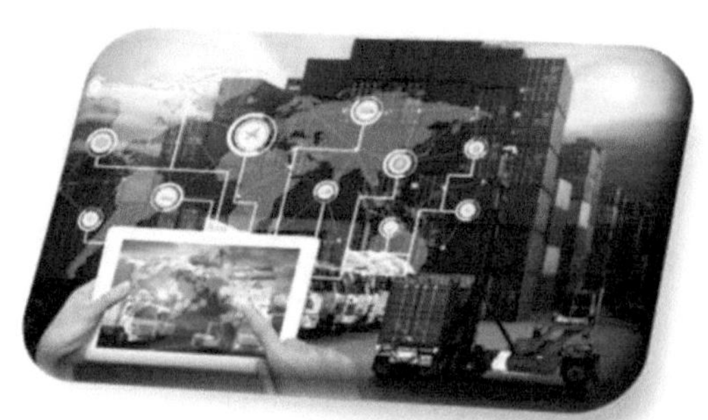

P21 - R001

2. Manufacturing

Customer Service
Once the product is ordered and entered into the seller's system, the product undergoes the manufacturing, sourcing, and delivery process. On the seller's side, customer service helps buyers or customers with questions about the order, delivery dates, status of fabrication, concerns or problems with a product, or warranty issues.

Expediting
On the buyer's side, supply chain teams use expeditors and quality surveyors to verify that the order will be delivered as promised and with the quality and requirements expected.

Quality Surveillance
Quality surveyors visit sellers' factories to verify that the products comply with the requirements of the order. Surveyors check whether the manufacturers are using the right material, color, and texture.

3. Warehousing

Another vital component in the supply chain is warehousing. When products or goods are shipped from the factory and are not yet ready to reach a store or else require storage for some time or to be redirected to another place, they are sent to warehouses or distribution centers. Warehouses or distribution centers vary in size depending on the number of goods or products they handle. Pallets holding products or goods are organized and stored in racks.

Warehousing activities include the following:

- Quality control receipt inspection
- Receiving and allocation
- Documentation and receiving reports
- Damage, shortages, and deficiencies resolution
- Laydown area planning
- Safety and security

P23 - R001

4. Distribution – Logistics

Just Imagine that you buy some chairs in Japan and you need to ship them to your house or store in the USA, Canada, or another part of the world. To do this, you need the help of logistics. The primary objective of logistics is to transport products in the timeliest, most cost-effective, and safest manner possible. Logistics will provide carrier selection and coordination to ensure that shipments of products or goods arrive safely and on time.

Logistics face many challenges around the world, and to solve these challenges logistics teams, freight forwarders, and carriers need to be proactive on identifying potential delays or changes in regulations, routes, or safety. In addition, logistics teams need to find opportunities to consolidate cargo where possible, prepare cargo for maximum stowage, and verify that proper packing methods are used to reduce the risk of damage during transit. Products or goods are shipped in boxes, cargo containers, pallets, export packing, or any other form of packing that will guarantee that the product will arrive in perfect condition.

The principal modes of transportation are as follows:

Rail

The use of rail is associated with containerized cargo, as containers are picked up from and/or delivered to either the closest CY (container yard) or CFS (container freight station). Rail is normally used to facilitate unloading operations without having any further negative impact on the local community.

Motor Freight (Inland)

For inland or motor freight, multiple routes for transporting the products to the delivery location need to be evaluated and considered. Depending on the type of products, a route survey may be required to ensure that a route is suitable for transport. Route surveys provide specific information and identify potential obstructions that will need to be removed or altered to allow the movement of the cargo. Routes are dictated by the governing body over the roads, whether that is state, county, or municipality.

Truckload

Types of truckloads are as follows:

1. Less than truckloads (LTLs)

LTLs consist of small shipments such as pallets, boxes, or skids. LTL shipments are not shipped via dedicated trucks; instead they are shipped through a system of terminals. This allows for a reduction in cost; however, transit times are longer.

2. Full truckloads (FTLs)

FTLs are used on full deck trailers. FTLs are shipped via dedicated trucks from the point of origin to the destination.

3. Over dimensional loads (OD loads)

OD loads consist of anything that breaks a boundary on a legal load, be it weight or dimension. A legal standard load is 48’ L × 8’6” W × 13’6” H (loaded height) and 40,000 pounds. OD loads require permits for transport, and depending upon the piece, these permits can take extended periods of time to secure. Some permits will require specific routing based on weight or dimensions.

Air Freight

Air freight is generally to be avoided when shipping sizable items to minimize transportation costs. Air freight is recommended when one or more of the following is true:

- It is less costly than ocean or inland freight.
- The components or products are urgently required to meet schedule and demand.
- Overnight shipments are required.

Ocean Freight

Containers and flat racks are used on ocean shipments for smaller or larger items that are suitable for containerization or are just beyond the limits of a container. Shipping via ocean containers provides more security and safety during transit and allows one to reduce costs. Standard shipping containers are 8 feet (2.43 meters) wide and 8.5 feet (2.59 meters) high, and they come in two lengths: 20 feet (6.06 meters) and 40 feet (12.2 meters). A ship can carry up to 18,000 containers.

There is no limit to size or weight. Carriers (airplanes, ships, trucks, and trains) have the capacity to transport any kind of goods or products (houses, cars, animals, liquids, or gases). In any case, carriers use shipping bar codes, symbols, and Incoterms to track and coordinate the shipment all along its route until it is delivered. Cargo symbols provide safety and handling instructions. Shipping bar codes provide information about origin, destination, weight; a tracking number; and sellers' and buyers' information.

Estimated transit times (Example)

North America (Truckload) From/To	Europe (Ocean Freight to USA)	Asia (Ocean Freight to USA)
West Coast 5 days East Coast 5 days	Break-bulk vessel - 60 days Europe container vessel - 45 days	Break-bulk vessel - 84 days Container vessel - 60 days

International Shipping Terms (Incoterms)

The Incoterms or International Commercial Terms are a series of terms published by the International Chamber of Commerce (ICC) relating to international commercial law. The most common are the following:

1. Domestic Shipping Terms

FCA (Free Carrier) Seller's Facility

FCA Seller's Facility is used on domestic shipments. FCA Named Place means the seller delivers the goods to the carrier nominated by the buyer at the named place. This places the responsibility for loading the material onto the buyer's equipment on the seller.

2. International Shipping Terms

FAS (Free Alongside Ship) Named Port of Shipment

FAS means that the seller has completed his or her obligation to deliver when he or she has cleared as goods for export and that the goods are placed alongside the vessel at the named port of shipment.

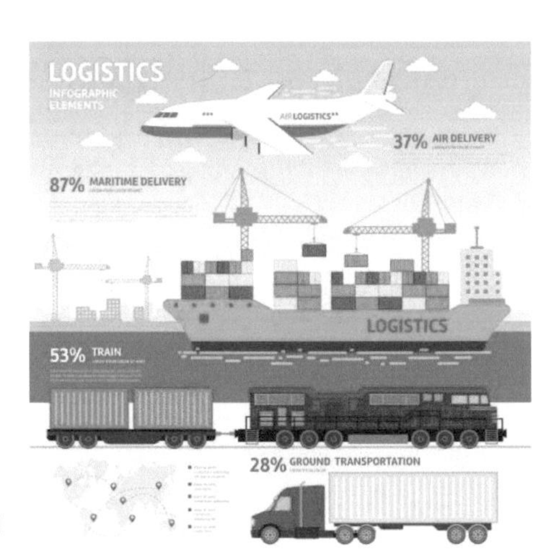

P27 - R001

FOB (Free on Board) Named Port of Shipment

FOB means that the seller has completed his or her obligation to deliver when he or she has cleared the goods for export and the goods pass the ship's rail at the named port of shipment.

DDP (Destination Duty Paid) Seller's Facility

DDP means that the seller is responsible for delivering the goods to the named place in the buyer's country and for paying all costs in bringing the goods to the destination, including import duties.

Freight Forwarder / Customs Broker

Freight forwarders or customs brokers are responsible for export customs clearance when required, import customs clearance, payment of duties, value added taxes (VAT), and other legal requirements.

5. Delivery

Product delivery around the world is now focusing on new technology, and there is going to be a paradigm shift. Drone delivery is now a reality in some suburban areas, and tests continue in large cities or in places with difficult access. As drone technology advances, online retailers will become more interested in using drones as an option that provides faster delivery, cost reduction, and safety. Current restrictions on airspace limit the use of this technology, but in the future, and with changes and adjustments to laws

and regulations, drone delivery is expected to satisfy customer demands for fast delivery. Autonomous cars are also part of the supply chain and logistics future.

P29 - R001

P29 - R002

Smart Goals

Supply chain professionals need to have the capacity to plan, anticipate, or forecast issues that can affect efficiency and performance. They must identify new scenarios, restrictions, and areas of opportunity, have playbook thinking, and play smart.

Goal	Activities
Specific	Identify Goals Identify Needs Use a Design Thinking Approach
Measure	Measure Progress based on established parameters
Achieve	Objectives are reasonable. What do we need to achieve them?
Define	Define strategies Use Critical Thinking
Implement	How long will it take to accomplish goals? Holistic Thinking

Design Thinking
Use a design approach to solve problems and generate ideas, implement, and test

Critical Thinking
Analysis of facts to make innovative decisions based on standards of excellence.

Holistic Thinking
See things as a whole, including the relationships between the elements in a complex system.

Supply Chain in Various Industries

Now that we have learned the basics about the supply chain, we are going to look at how these concepts apply to specific industries.

Supply Chain in the Food Industry

The supply chain in the food industry is considered to be the number one supply chain in the world. As people are more concerned about health and implementing better food habits, the supply chain needs to evolve and be ready for the challenge to transport food faster with less handling and meet the safety norms and requirements. Sustainability is the word that brings together supply chain and the activities of and new strategies in the food industry.

Sustainability is about taking care of the environment. This means that producers (e.g., farmers) and animal products (e.g., meat and milk) need to work with supply chain teams to find better ways to manage and handle food products.

Food industry supply chain challenges include the following:

1. Meeting the daily demand for tons of fresh food
2. Reduced consumer interest in packaged and processed food
3. Reduced transit time between farms and grocery stores and consumers
4. Maintaining the freshness of food with the use of organic technology
5. Implementing and developing innovative distribution methods

The food industry is evolving, and as part of this evolution—and to provide better products (organic/fresh) to consumers—urban/community farming is now becoming a new trend. This is a good opportunity for supply chain teams and future generations to show the value of the supply chain professional as a contributor to innovation. Remember that supply chain needs to be in constant evolution to face new challenges.

The Michelin Star and Supply Chain

The Michelin star and the Michelin Guide have an interesting relationship with supply chain. The Michelin star is the most recognized award for excellence in restaurants and cuisine; the Michelin star originated with the publication of the Michelin Guide. In 1900, bike tire manufacturers Edouard and Andre Michelin had the idea to manufacture replacement tires for cars. However, the idea turned out to be negative because the need or demand for new tires was very low. At that time people used a car only to drive short distances. The tires had no wear and therefore lasted a long time. For this reason, the Michelin brothers developed the Michelin Guide providing information like maps, tire repair and replacement instructions, and the locations of hotels, restaurants, and gasoline stations throughout France. The guide was a big success, and as a consequence of its contents, people increased their use of cars and drove longer

distances. That helped the Michelin brothers to sell more replacement tires; and more tires required a better supply chain structure.

In 1926, the Michelin Guide began to award stars for fine dining establishments, as follows:

One (1) Michelin star: a very good restaurant in its category.
Two (2) Michelin stars: excellent cooking, worth a detour.
Three (3) Michelin stars: exceptional cuisine, worth a special journey.

Every year when the guide is published, it generates speculation and debate about which restaurants might lose, a Michelin star and which might gain a Michelin star.

Opportunity to Innovate

Every day 20 to 40 percent of fresh produce is thrown away because it does not meet retailers' standards for appearance. This ugly produce is still rich in nutrients, and many organizations are looking for ways to sell these fruits and vegetables that would otherwise be thrown away. As a future supply chain professional, how can you contribute to solve this problem?

Supply Chain in the Retail Industry

Supply chain in the retail industry (shops, finished goods or products) is not as sophisticated as in the food industry; however, given the increasing demand of products by consumers around the world, it also requires constant innovation to reduce transit times, reduce transit costs, and avoid the need for keeping high inventory (large amounts of products in warehouses, shops, or distribution centers). Finished products are sent to warehouses or distribution centers, and from there they are distributed to stores or directly to customers.

Online shopping is transforming the industry as retailers prefer to send products to clients directly and not to the stores; this is helping to reduce inventory and operating costs. With the help of logistics, retailers provide customers information in real time about their order/product location and projected delivery dates and times.

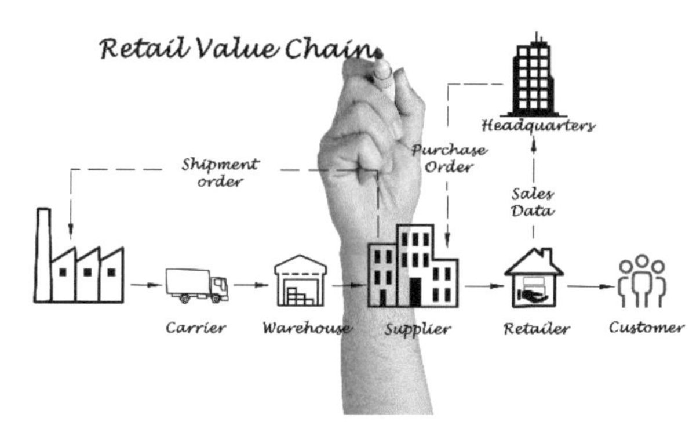

P34 - R001

Customer service is an important piece of this effort, as customer service representatives need to provide answers and options to clients. In some cases, if a product is lost or arrives late, the customer service representative will offer a refund or a free exchange.

Supply Chain in the Engineering and Construction Industry (EPC)

The engineering and construction industry oversees the engineering and construction of industrial projects (e.g., refineries, chemical plants, power plants, and mines) around the world. Supply chain or procurement is a component of this industry in charge of the purchasing (sourcing), transportation, and delivery of all the equipment, and/or materials required at projects. Supply chain in this industry is now facing numerous challenges, like constant changes in market conditions, client budget restrictions, tight schedules, and fierce competition. All these challenges increase the pressure on supply chain teams, which are expected to perform with better and enhanced efficiency.

The supply chain function in the EPC industry can play a significant role in the success of EPC firms; however, it is still seen as an administrative discipline that does not require major skills or employee training, or its development is limited to learning in-house old-school procedures. Some organizations are now recognizing the value of supply chain as a discipline that contributes to the organization innovation processes and that helps reduce costs through the implementation of integrated solutions for clients. In the next five to ten years EPC companies will require a new generation of supply chain professionals with agility, adaptability, and critical-thinking skills.

In the EPC industry supply chain teams are usually managed by individuals with many years in the industry and an understanding of the methods through lessons learned, but with no scholar base or outside of the industry experience. Team members follow these individuals because of their “know how” (tacit knowledge) of proved old practices and habits, learning from them by observation, and then by continuous practice; working in automatic without applying critical, holistic, or design thinking to their work.

Strategic Change required for Supply Chain

The key of change in supply chain is to increase the level of professionalism and competence in the individuals through the implementation of organic practices and procedures that will allow individuals to use creative and critical thinking. Old procedures and policies instruct workers only to follow them, but not to challenge them, creating repetitive (by memory) and by routine operations that do not add value.

Options to Address Change

Determine the tolerance for change. Each organization or project is different and requires a different approach and strategy. It is important to assess the context before implementing new changes, to define a plan that will maximize acceptance and minimize objections.

Look for ideas at every level. The best ideas normally come from the individuals that are doing the job on a daily basis, and not from top management. Individuals need to be encouraged to share improvement ideas and opportunities as part of the daily activities.

Encourage value-added work. Operate more effectively through value-added work and a change mentality, reduce the amount of routine work, and set higher challenges for the team (implement higher-level work that cannot be automated, work that requires expertise or skilled judgment).

P37 - R001

One major challenge for the supply chain in this industry is that projects are normally located in deserted or isolated areas around the world; these challenge increase risks, costs, and delivery times, and also affect the preservation and maintenance of equipment and materials on-site. If a material or piece of equipment is late, the project could be delayed. In such an event, the project will cost more, and the client will not be satisfied.

The Supply Chain
PLAYBOOK

Summary

I hope that you liked *The Supply Chain Playbook* and that I have helped to awaken your curiosity and interest in supply chain. One of the major problems in the supply chain discipline is the lack of talent. The US Bureau of Labor Statistics (2017) reported that the requirement for qualified supply chain professionals would increase by 22 percent between 2012 and 2022. A study by the Florida Institute of Technology (FIT) in 2017 suggested that it is becoming more difficult to find supply chain leaders with expert-level skills and talent.

The supply chain discipline is becoming more important and of immense value to different industries and companies around the world. If you decide to follow this career path, do so with passion and respect. It is a profession that requires constant learning, development of skills, and evolution. It requires commitment to reach excellence, to think differently, and to innovate. In any industry, supply chain is going to give you the opportunity to face difficult challenges or scenarios. You cannot be the best if you do not face situations that will force you to use all your skills, expertise, and knowledge.

In an extremely competitive environment, continuous improvement is a necessary element of organizational success. To address change supply chain professionals, need to have a leading transformation mentality by using and developing critical, design and holistic thinking, adapting to change, analyzing what others are doing, and learning from supply chain world leaders or innovators. As leaders, we need to improve the capacity of our teams to work smarter through collaboration, facilitate knowledge creation and transfer, attract, retain, motivate and recognize knowledgeable workers, and be aware of our responsibility for the human capital and intellectual assets that we have on hand.

Success does not stop with your highest goal; it continues and evolves in the same way we evolve.

Horacio Sanchez

Glossary

autonomous: Existing independent of anything else (not directly operated by a human).

bid: An offer or quote provided by a supplier or vendor upon request.

bid summary: A commercial analysis that summarizes a bid or a quote and sets the recommendation for purchase.

buyer: A person employed to select and purchase products or goods.

commercial terms: The terms and conditions (payment, delivery, warranty, and shipping terms) of a purchase order.

critical thinking: The objective analysis of facts to form a judgment.

delivery: The transfer of products or goods from supplier to receiver or consignee.

EPC (engineering, procurement, and construction): An industry that provides professional services including preparation of plans, drawings and specifications, procurement of all or part of the material requirements, and construction of the scope of facilities.

equipment: An item designed or chosen to perform a specific processing function.

Glossary

Incoterms: The Incoterms or International Commercial Terms are a series of predefined commercial terms published by the International Chamber of Commerce (ICC) relating to international commercial law.

logistics: A term associated with the movement and storage of materials.

PO (purchase order): A formally documented agreement for the acquisition of materials, equipment, goods, or services.

quotation: A statement of price, terms of sale, and description of goods or services offered by a supplier to a prospective buyer; a bid.

receiving: Taking delivery of an item at a designated location.

RFQ (request for quotation): A document sent by the buyer or purchasing department to suppliers listing item descriptions and quantities. Suppliers respond to the inquiry by indicating their interest in bidding on the items by quoting prices.

requisition: The document or set of documents that describe what is required, how much, the quality required, when, and where.

surveyor: A person whose occupation is to verify that the requirements (size, color, etc.) are being followed as requested.

Index

Photo Credits:

Page 2
P2-R001: Strategy plan hand drawn outline doodle icon - iStock- RaStudio -ID 1014991968

Page 3
P3-R001: Tactic vector icon. Flat design - iStock- Marko Babii - ID 984369746

Page 10
P10-R001: White-collar worker - a-r-t-i-s-t/Collection: iStock/Thinkstock 486933767

Page 13
P13-R001: White-collar worker - a-r-t-i-s-t/Collection: iStock/Thinkstock 486933767

Page 16
P16-R001: White-collar worker - a-r-t-i-s-t/Collection: iStock/Thinkstock 486933767

Page 17
P17-R001: White-collar worker - a-r-t-i-s-t/Collection: iStock/Thinkstock 486933767

Page 21
P21-R001: Hand holding tablet is pressing button on touch screen - iStock - 801087372

Index

Photo Credits (Cont.):

Page 23
P23-R001: Moderm warehouse - iStock -ID 478287820

Page 27
P27-R001: Logistics and transportation infographic elements - iStock - ID 501857088

Page 29
P29-R001: Drone with remote control flying over city - iStock - ID 667226100
P29-R002: Delivery drone flying in city - iStock - ID 641135686

Page 31
P31-R001: Coffee plantation landscape - iStock - ID 671431126

Page 34
P34-R001: Retail value chain - iStock - ID 533611085

Page 35
P35-R001: Industrial Chemical Plant Isolated - Serz72 - iStock -Thinkstock -547044378

Page 37
P37-R001: Oil refinery - Petrochemical plant – iStock - ID 457328841

Index

References

1. Bureau of Labor Statistics, U.S. Department of Labor, Occupational Outlook Handbook, 2016-17 Edition, Logisticians, on the Internet at https://www.bls.gov/ooh/business-and-financial/logisticians.htm

2. Florida Tech University, (2017). Supply Chain Skills Evolving, Growing in Demand. https://www.floridatechonline.com/. Retrieved from: http://floridatech-blog.herokuapp.com/blog/process-improvement/supply-chain-skills-evolving-growing-in-demand/

The Supply Chain
PLAYBOOK

About the Author

Horacio Sanchez is an architect and currently a supply chain manager at an engineering and construction firm. He is passionate about leadership, supply chain, and design thinking. At the age of five, he was convinced that architecture was his passion and the career that he wanted to follow. However, twenty years ago, supply chain crossed his path, and since then he has dedicated his time to evolving as a supply chain professional with a design, critical-thinking, and holistic-thinking philosophy. In *The Supply Chain Playbook*, Horacio Sanchez shares his experiences and concepts learned during his twenty-one years of cross-industry international supply chain expertise.

As a transformational leader, Horacio Sanchez likes to mentor and encourage new generations of supply chain professionals, emphasizing the importance of constant learning, evolution, and the commitment to look for situations that require the use of full thinking, analysis, and reasoning.

Horacio Sanchez lives in Houston, Texas, with his wife and three children. This is his second book written for young people. His first book, *Architecture for Kids*, was a great learning experience.

Printed in the United States
By Bookmasters